IT'S TOUGH TO BE A KID

Walking Together Through Life's Tricky Moments

SNG EE PING

For my three lovely boys—Titus, Nate, and Elijah—the finest creations that God has blessed Elmer and me with.

KEY CHARACTERS

MAX, 11

PHOEBE, 12

STEPHANIE, 9

RICK, 8

CONTENTS

PROLOGUE

Chik . . . chik . . . chik . . . chik . . .

Stephanie jabbed her chisel at the tree trunk furiously as tears streamed down her cheeks.

It was a windy afternoon. The crisp, brown leaves fluttered around her and soft, pink petals landed on her hair and skirt. But, tucked away behind a flourishing undergrowth, she paid no attention to her surroundings. She continued to dig and scrape, pausing only to brush away the few strands of hair that kept sticking to her tear-stained face.

Finally, the chisel stopped, and she stared at her work: the small hollow in the tree trunk was finally a decent size. She stared at her hands—they were red and sore. She placed her chisel neatly into her toolbox, and took out a textbook from her bag.

Fresh tears pooled in Stephanie's eyes as she stared at the scribblings on the cover. She tore it out carefully, folded it, and stuffed it into the hollow. Now that the offending piece of paper was gone, she exhaled shakily, stood up, straightened her skirt, and brushed off the leaves and flowers. Then she picked up her school bag, took one last look at the tree, and continued walking home.

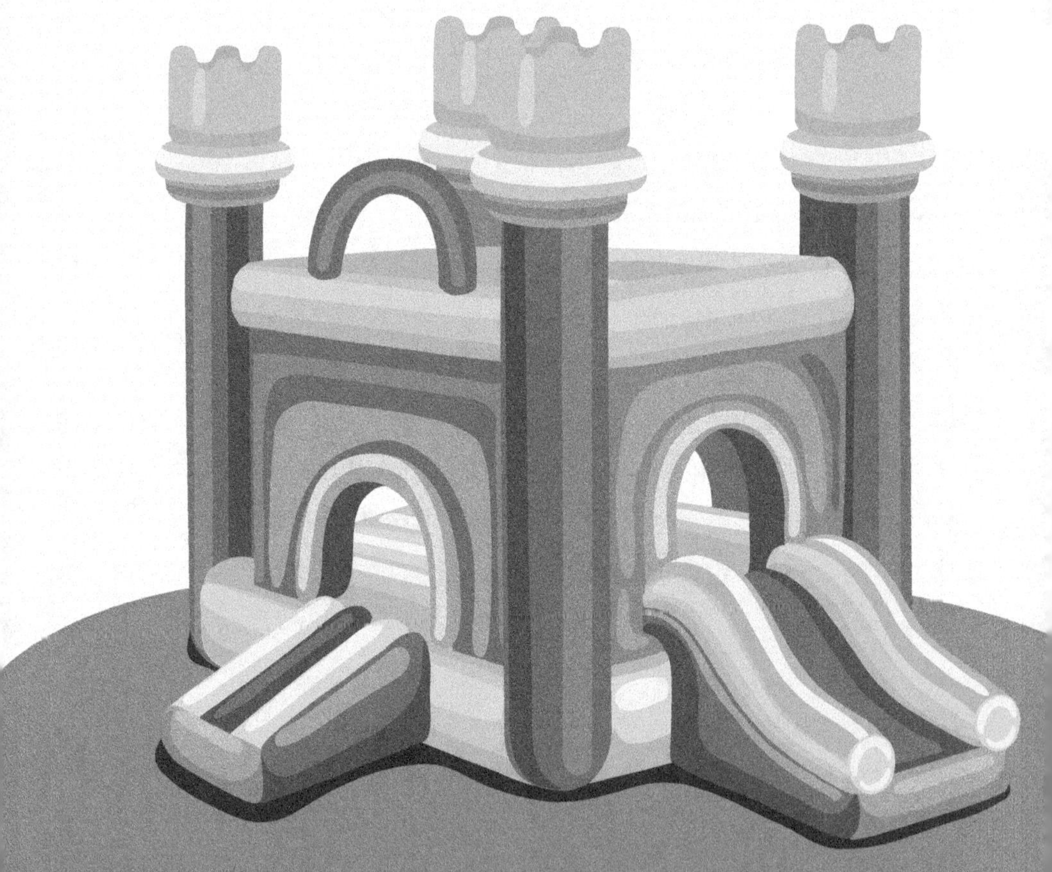

1
FINDERS KEEPERS

Riches that are gained by sinning aren't worth anything.
But doing what is right saves you from death.
—Proverbs 10:2

Every year on Children's Day, the school would be transformed into a massive carnival. An impressive bouncy castle, one-of-a-kind game stalls, mouth-watering food prepared by parents, and a whimsical-themed photo booth. It was the most anticipated event of the year. This year, the school was even giving out a special Star Wars-themed luggage tag for every ten coupons students bought.

Rick was bursting with excitement. An ardent Star Wars fan, he couldn't wait to receive his luggage tag. When his teacher finally called his name, Rick sped to the front of the class to collect his gift and coupons.

A Stormtrooper! Rick sighed, a little disappointed. He had hoped to get Darth Vader. He glanced around the class to see if there was anyone he could trade with.

Aha! A few tables away, he spotted Alden admiring the Darth Vader luggage tag that he'd just received. Rick slipped out of his seat while his teacher was still distributing the coupons and tags to the rest of the class, and asked if they could trade. Alden made a don't-you-dare-touch-mine face and swatted him away.

Rick scowled. He wanted the Darth Vader tag so badly, and could hardly concentrate during lessons. During recess, Rick had an idea. He sneaked past the watchful eyes of the prefects on duty and crept back into his classroom. He found the Darth Vader luggage tag in Alden's bag, pocketed it, and left his own Stormtrooper tag in its place.

As he was about to zip up Alden's bag, he saw a stack of carnival coupons on the floor. Rick counted and to his delight, there were $20 worth of coupons! Without thinking twice, he slipped the stack of coupons into his pocket.

When Rick reached home, he took out the luggage tag from his bag to show Mum.

"Mum, look what I have! A Darth Vader luggage tag! And I got my coupons today, too! You won't believe my luck. I found another $20 worth of coupons on the floor!" Rick exclaimed gleefully.

"The student who dropped those coupons must be very upset. It's probably one of your classmates. Wouldn't it be nice if you brought those coupons back and ask who lost them?" Mum suggested.

"No . . . finders keepers! Serves that person right for being so careless!" Rick retorted.

Just then, Mum's phone rang.

From across the room, Rick watched his mother's face grow more and more serious as she listened to the caller. When she hung up, she clasped the phone tightly in her hands and sat quietly in her chair.

Puzzled, Rick asked, "Mum, are you alright?"

"Mrs Choo just called," Mum said calmly. "Alden said you took his luggage tag, and he lost $20 worth of coupons, too."

"Well, I . . . I didn't take his. I merely traded mine with his. He didn't lose anything. As for the coupons, I found them on the floor," Rick muttered.

"Rick, remember the verse we read last night in Proverbs 10:2? It says that '*riches that are gained by sinning aren't worth anything. But doing what is right saves you from death.*' Did you trade Alden's luggage tag with his permission? If you didn't, that's stealing, son. And you might lose his friendship because of this."

Rick, who was looking down all the while, could feel his cheeks burning hot with shame. His eyes welled up with tears.

"Will Alden forgive me if I return them to him now?"

"Well, we'll see. We could go over now and return the tag and coupons if you are ready."

Rick wiped away his tears. The coupons and tag weighed heavily in his hands as he knocked on Alden's door. Mrs Choo welcomed them in with her usual smile, and gave Rick a reassuring nod.

Alden was playing with his troop of Star Wars figurines when Rick entered his room.

"Alden, I'm sorry I took your luggage tag. And I found your coupons near your bag, but I shouldn't have taken them. Will you forgive me?" Rick hung his head sheepishly.

"Of course, you are still my best buddy," Alden said easily. "You know, you can have the Darth Vader. I think I prefer the Stormtrooper anyway."

Rick looked up, stunned. Alden was a much better friend than he was. He mumbled, "Thanks Alden."

"No problem! Wanna play?"

Doing the right thing has definitely saved our friendship from death, Rick thought, as he settled on the floor to arrange a fleet of Star Wars spacecraft fighters.

23 OCT
WELCOME TO
BOUNCY
CASTLE
S$20
BOUNCY CASTLE

2
WISDOM AND SHAME

When pride comes, shame follows.
But wisdom comes to those who are not proud.
—Proverbs 11:2

One afternoon, Alden came over to Rick's house to play.

"How did you do on the English test?" Rick asked.

"Just passed," replied Alden sullenly.

"Mrs Kamal said I wrote well," Rick said gleefully.

"Good for you," mumbled Alden, looking down at his feet.

"Actually, it was pretty easy," boasted Rick, not realising that Alden was actually feeling glum. "Mrs Kamal even said I should be able to enter the best class next year."

"Everyone wants to enter the best class. I hope I can go too," Alden sighed.

Mum overheard their conversation, and after Alden left, she spoke to Rick. "You know, 'When pride comes, shame *follows. But wisdom comes to those who are not proud.'* I'm glad you did well, but did you realise you might have been a little boastful? Did you notice Alden's disappointment with his results?"

"But I like to do well, and I also like others to know that I've done well. Those words just came out of my mouth. I couldn't help it," Rick defended himself.

"We can control our words if we stop and think before we speak," Mum suggested. "Pride makes us selfish, and we think only about ourselves and not others. This is how we end up hurting people, like how you've hurt Alden."

"Alright, Mum."

The following day, Mrs Kamal gave the class a project: "Saving our Planet." The best project was to be featured in the school's magazine. The students were to choose a partner to work with. Alden chose Rick, but Rick wanted to work with Ben, the smartest boy in class.

The following week, the students brought their projects for submission. Alden's project was the most outstanding: an elaborate 3D clay model of a battered-looking earth, with several flaps that could be lifted to reveal facts about climate change. He and his partner had spent many gruelling hours after school for an entire week to work on it.

That day, Alden found Rick crying in the classroom during recess.

"Rick, why are you crying?"

"Ben hasn't done his part for the project. He says I'm too dumb and he's not going to work with me. I should have worked with you instead. And now I've nothing to show Mrs Kamal."

"You should tell Mrs Kamal about Ben. We can also ask Mrs Kamal for more time. Come, I'll go with you."

In the end, Ben and Rick were given till the end of the week. Alden stayed with them during recess over the next few days to complete the project. Rick's heart was filled with both gratitude and shame.

After submitting his project, Rick told Mum what had happened.

"I didn't want to work with Alden as I was afraid he would pull me down. But then, when Alden submitted a very impressive project with his partner, I realised I had been too proud of myself. Alden didn't blame me and even helped me work with Ben to complete the project. He's such a good friend, Mum."

"He is indeed. Shall we invite him for dinner tonight to thank him?"

"Yes. I'd love to!"

3
THE TRUMPET TREE

The fruit that godly people bear is like a tree of life.
And those who are wise save lives.
—Proverbs 11:30

"Hey, pass me my worksheet!" shouted Rick. Simon rolled his eyes and stuck his tongue out at him.

"Get your dirty hands off my table! If you do this again, I'm going to tell the teacher."

But Simon just pushed his chair back forcefully. It hit Rick's desk, knocking his palette over and splashing paint all over his artwork.

Rick was furious. His painting, which he'd been carefully working on all morning, was ruined. He couldn't understand why his form teacher, Mrs Lim, wouldn't let him change his seat, no matter how many times he'd requested to.

She had even coaxed him to show Simon more understanding! Unbelievable . . .

Back home, Rick couldn't help but whine, "Dad, have you met someone as annoying as Simon?"

"Yep!" Dad said.

Rick raised his brows and waited for Dad to continue.

"There was a boy called Don in my class. He made strange comments in class and never knew when to stop asking questions. Our teachers told us he was special and wanted us to be more understanding. But he was so annoying that most of us avoided him. Some boys even teased him pretty badly."

"Did you tease him too, Dad?" Rick asked, wide-eyed at the thought of his father, whom he admired, being mean to anyone.

"Yes, unfortunately. I didn't understand why Don behaved the way he did. But one day, my Sunday school teacher shared a verse from Proverbs 11:30: '*The fruit that godly people bear is like a tree of life. And those who are wise save lives,*'" Dad said. I remember staring out of the window in class, and seeing a trumpet tree in its full bloom, exploding with pink flowers. It was quite beautiful. I wondered what it would mean for a person to 'bear fruit' like a tree.

"The next day, Don suddenly screamed in the middle of our English lesson. He started banging his forehead on the desk as if he was possessed. Then suddenly, he stood up, lifted his chair over his head, and glared angrily at his partner, Keong."

Dad continued: "Apparently, Keong had been making fun of him. I was sitting in front of them, and without thinking, stood up to grab the chair from Don. Don stared at me, huffing heavily, with his fists tightly clenched. No one knew what he would do next. But something prompted me to do a surprising thing. I grasped Don's fists gently but firmly, and held his seething gaze. It seemed to work and I felt his body relax."

"You saved Keong from being hit!" Rick gasped, enthralled.

"Yes, I believe God was guiding me that day. After the incident, I was appointed the official buddy for Don. I got to know Don better, and discovered that he had an awesome memory and was a math whiz. You should get to know Simon better, too."

"Not going to happen," said Rick, shaking his head.

The following day, while Rick was dashing to the field for a game of soccer with his friends during recess, he noticed Simon sitting alone at the stairs, mumbling to himself. Rick felt sorry for him and shouted, "Hey dude, want to join us for soccer?"

Simon's eyes lit up, and he got up immediately and ran after Rick. Simon turned out to be an excellent goalkeeper.

A week later, it was the mid-year parent-teacher meeting. Rick and his parents waited outside the classroom, while Mrs Lim was speaking to Simon and his parents. A moment later, she requested for Rick and his parents to enter the classroom. Simon's parents beamed with delight when they saw Rick.

"Mr and Mrs Tan, these are Simon's parents, and they would like to thank your son for being a good friend to Simon," explained Mrs Lim.

"So you're Rick! You've been looking out for Simon. Thank you so much," said Simon's father. "He has special needs, you see. Most people don't understand his behaviour, and choose to stay away from him. But recently, he told us that he has a good friend in class, so we wanted to meet you to thank you personally. We're very grateful to you, Rick."

Turning to Rick's parents, Simon's father continued, "You must be so proud of your son!"

"Yes. Rick's my best friend!" Simon looked at Rick, flashing his goofy smile and baring the gaps of his missing baby teeth. Rick was embarrassed, but his heart swelled with pride. He shot a glance at Dad and caught the glimmer of pride on his face.

The following day, as Rick was walking home with his brother Max, he noticed the pink flowers that littered the pavement they were on. He looked up, and was delighted to see some trumpet trees in full bloom. It was a splendid sight.

He remembered the verse that Dad had quoted: "*The fruit that godly people bear is like a tree of life. And those who are wise save lives.*" Suddenly, it made sense to him. He had borne the fruit of kindness that had helped Simon. And just like how it was a delight to see a tree in bloom, he realised that a person who bore fruit would bring joy to himself and to others, too. He recalled the pride on Dad's face, and felt joy stirring in his heart.

As he walked closer to a trumpet tree, Rick saw something shifting behind the thick undergrowth beside the tree and heard some noises:

Chik . . . chik . . . chik . . . chik . . .

Was it a wild dog? A python? A ghost? Rick and Max shuddered, and ran all the way home.

4

PET ANTS

You people who don't want to work, think about the ant!

Consider its ways and be wise!

It has no commander.

It has no leader or ruler.

But it stores up its food in summer.

It gathers its food at harvest time.

—Proverbs 6:6–8

One evening, the Tan family gathered for family devotion.

"I bought some pets for you," Dad said, placing a formicarium, or ant farm, on the table.

"An ant colony! How fascinating," exclaimed Max.

"Why would anyone want to keep them as pets? They look creepy," said Phoebe in disgust.

"Look! That must be the queen ant," cried Stephanie. "Does she command them, Dad?"

"No one commands them. They are self-organised, and are excellent team players. Proverbs 6:6–8 mentions these diligent workers. Phoebe, can you read the verses to us?" Dad asked.

"'You people who don't want to work, think about the ant! Consider its ways and be wise! It has no commander. It has no leader or ruler. But it stores up its food in summer. It gathers its food at harvest time'," she recited.

The children watched the ants at work. One brought a crumb, which was larger than its body, to its nest, while another sped off to pick up more food. Soon, ants were moving back and forth, carrying crumbs.

"They're so busy. And they look so organised, too," observed Stephanie.

"Yes, they don't need instructions. And look at these ants here. They are feeding the baby ants. Each ant just goes around and works faithfully," said Dad.

Seeing his children so captivated by the ants' working habits, Dad took the opportunity to ask, "Kids, we've been rostered this Sunday to take care of the pre-schoolers while their parents go for Bible study. We'll have to think of a craft and some games to engage the children. Phoebe and Max, could both of you think of some ideas and delegate some duties to Ricky and Stephanie? Shall we work like the ants?"

"Surely we're better than the ants!" exclaimed Max.

It was Sunday morning. The children chattered noisily in the car. Stephanie, though, was rather silent, staring out the window as the car whizzed past the cluster of trumpet trees near their school.

The Tan family soon arrived at church, and were hurriedly unloading the bags from the car when Phoebe exclaimed, "Hey Max, where's our bag of craft and games?"

"Oh, I thought you took them," replied Max.

"I told you to take them. You don't remember anything I say!" Phoebe screamed.

"Hey, you spent a long time getting dressed this morning! I was the one scrambling around for the items. And all you did was boss me around!" Max shouted back angrily.

"Excuse me! I stayed up last night to prepare the craft materials while you were sleeping. Now what're we going to do with the children?" Phoebe said, almost in tears.

"Stop arguing. You'll have to think of something later for the children. Let's go in now. We're late," said Dad furiously.

After church was over, Dad asked Phoebe and Max, "What happened this morning? Why were you so disorganised?"

"Nobody wanted to take the lead at first, so the discussion didn't take place till Saturday night," said Max.

"We kept thinking we still had time; then Saturday came, and we still had no plans," confessed Phoebe.

Dad caught sight of the formicarium on the shelf behind them. "What did you learn about the ants last week that could help you do better the next time?" he asked.

"The ants store food in summer so they'll have enough for winter. We need to plan ahead and not work at the last minute," reflected Max.

"We should work together as a team. Sorry for being bossy, Max," said Phoebe.

Dad said, "Now, here's your second chance. Christmas is coming. Mum and I think we should bless some neighbours. I would like Phoebe and Max to plan and prepare the gifts for distribution. Do you think you can do that?"

"Yes," chorused the two.

"I'll help," volunteered Rick.

"I'll help, too!" Stephanie chirped.

5
FAR RICHER

One person gives freely but gets even richer.
Another person doesn't give what they should but gets even poorer.
—Proverbs 11:24

Christmas was just a week away. Phoebe and Max had already planned and purchased the items. Like busy ants, everyone in the family helped to pack them into bags. The day before distribution, at least 20 bags were packed to the brim with an assortment of groceries sitting in neat rows on the floor.

Phoebe had suggested purchasing the gifts with their savings. So, the week before the distribution, the children had carefully counted all their savings. It came to a tidy sum of $100. But Max did not want to put in all his savings. He secretly stashed away $20 for the comic books he planned to buy.

"Kids, we'll distribute these bags to some families tomorrow. Hopefully, it'll bring them some cheer. Phoebe and Max, thanks for organising this, and everyone else for helping," announced Dad.

The Tan family had an early start the next morning. The children were excited to give out the goodie bags to the families who needed them. But Max trudged along with the heavy bags, trailing behind sullenly.

When they arrived at the block and entered the lift, they were greeted by a stench of urine. Max immediately held his breath and pinched his nose grumpily, even more convinced that he shouldn't have come along.

Once the lift doors opened, he lunged forward and dramatically took in a deep breath of air. But the air outside was equally stale. Along the dim corridor, styrofoam boxes with bits of food still in them were lying beside random piles of shoes, prams, old toys, wooden shelves, old pillows, and mattresses.

As the Tan family walked along the narrow corridor, they passed many gates that were chained with heavy locks. The absence of shoes or slippers suggested that the flats were vacant. But they soon came upon a woman in a long floral print dress, trying to put out a long bamboo pole with laundry.

"Hello," Mum called cheerfully. "We'd like to offer you a gift." The woman eyed them suspiciously, as though trying to decide if they were scammers. But as Mum held out the bag of goodies to her, the woman smiled, and received it with a word of thanks.

The children met many people that morning: a jovial and portly man in a white singlet and shorts who shoved drinks into their hands as he thanked them profusely for the gifts. An elderly lady who hobbled to the door with her walker, smiling at them toothlessly as she collected a bag. A young mother carrying a baby, with three other small children skipping playfully around her, her tired eyes lighting up as she spied milk powder in one of the bags.

Arriving at the final flat of the morning, the children met their father's colleague, Sam, a security guard who worked at their dad's office building. He was celebrating his daughter's birthday with his family, but warmly welcomed them in.

The living room was small but clean, dressed in simple furnishings. Two huge cardboard boxes were flipped over to serve as tables. There was a bed at the end of the living room, just outside the kitchen, with at least four mattresses stacked on top of each other.

Looking embarrassed, Sam said, "I hope you don't mind. We usually sit on the floor for our meals." He looked around anxiously for some stools and chairs to offer them.

"Please don't worry. We're sorry to disturb your celebration," Mum quickly offered.

Sam's wife, who was from Thailand, was equally hospitable, ushering them to sit and help themselves to the food. She had whipped up a feast for her daughter's birthday. There was fried rice, green curry chicken, tom yum seafood soup, fried vermicelli, and mango salad.

"My wife has cooked enough to feed a village! Come, here, help yourself with the food," Sam said cheerfully.

Famished, the Tan family sat down at the table. The food was delicious, and everyone enjoyed themselves. Even Max, who had till then been feeling unhappy, was delighted with the sumptuous treat. After the meal, everyone savoured the cake and desserts that Sam's wife had prepared.

As they left Sam's house later that afternoon, Stephanie hung onto her father's arm and said, "I feel quite rich today, Dad. My heart feels full."

Phoebe added, "Yeah, same. I felt quite poor when I gave up my savings, and almost regretted making the suggestion for us to purchase gifts with our savings. But I feel like I received so much more today. It feels really good to be able to help people, and to make new friends."

Dad smiled, heartened. "You know, that's exactly what Proverbs 11:24 means when it says: '*One person gives freely but get even richer. Another person doesn't give what they should but gets even poorer.*' Being rich doesn't only mean having more wealth and possessions, but finding priceless things like love, relationships, and peace. Think of how much poorer we would have been today, if you kids hadn't given up your savings freely."

At this, Max burst into tears. Everyone looked at him, startled. "I . . . I . . . I kept some money to buy comic books," he sobbed. I had saved up for so many months . . . all my friends have them.

"I didn't want to come today because I hated that I had to give my money away to people I didn't know. But . . . but now I feel terrible . . . Sam's family didn't have much, but they were so happy to share their lunch with us. And I couldn't even give up $20!" he wailed, dissolving into more sobs.

Putting his arms around Max, Dad spoke softly, "It's alright, son. Everyone makes mistakes. I'm glad that you've learnt how keeping the money for yourself doesn't always make you richer."

6
STRAIGHT AHEAD

A person who has no sense enjoys doing foolish things.
But a person who has understanding walks straight ahead.
—Proverbs 15:21

After recess, Stephanie returned to class to prepare for lessons. She took out her English textbook, and was shocked to see scribbles in neon colours splashed across the cover.

Cry baby

Pale face

Weak

Mousy

At the centre of the cover was a drawing of Bugs Bunny. She knew it was to mock her protruding front teeth, and the bunny's long floppy ears were meant to look like her two long ponytails.

Stephanie looked up, and saw Chloe and her friends observing her. Their giggles and smirks felt like heavy punches, and caused a rising pain in her stomach. She tried to stop herself from crying, but a stubborn tear rolled down her cheek. *I am a cry baby. They're right.*

That day, it was Stephanie's turn to do show-and-tell. She rubbed her cold and clammy hands on her lap, and waited nervously for her turn. When her turn came, her voice came out as a whisper.

"Louder, please," the teacher called out.

Stephanie noticed the girls giggling and whispering behind their cupped hands over their mouths.

"Look! Her hands and legs are shaking."

"Nobody can hear."

"See how she rubs her nose."

"Looks so silly."

"Hope she ends soon."

Stephanie hastily ended her speech and asked for permission to go to the toilet. For the entire lesson, she locked herself in the cubicle and cried. *I am WEAK and MOUSY. They're right.*

After school, Stephanie avoided the usual path—a straight path along the canal that led to her flat—which most students used. She took a winding, gravelled path instead, one that cut through a field with thick undergrowth. Once shielded from other passers-by, she threw herself behind a trumpet tree and cried, the weight of the unhappy events of the day sinking in.

When she finally stood up to leave, she froze. Seconds later, she screamed and ran. She had caught sight of a lanky creature whose bright green skin blended with its surrounding. Stephanie managed to escape the slithery creature, but slipped on a muddy patch and landed hard on the gravel path. She hobbled home, wondering how she would explain her cuts and filth to Mum.

Her family was just getting ready for dinner when Stephanie finally made it home. As expected, her mother gasped at her state. But even before she could ask her daughter what had happened, Stephanie burst into tears.

Everyone stared at her, shocked. Mum quickly put her arms around her and hugged her tight. Like a waterlogged sponge being squeezed of its water, Stephanie blurted out everything that happened that day.

"Those girls have no sense. Like that verse Dad made us remember: '*A person who has no sense enjoys doing foolish things.*' Hey, do you want me to put my martial arts skills into good use and knock some sense into their heads?" Max offered, half-jokingly.

Stephanie giggled at her big brother in spite of herself. Through her sniffles, she asked, "Can you pray that I have darker skin and straighter teeth?"

Her parents exchanged worried looks. "It is not about changing your appearance, Steph," Mum said gently. "You need to show them that what *they* are doing is wrong. There is nothing wrong with how you look. God made you perfect, just the way you are."

"Mum's right. Remember the rest of Proverbs 15:16? '*A person who has understanding walks straight ahead,*'" said Dad. "If you understand that God loves you, and that we love you, you can walk through life with confidence. You're not alone, my dear."

He added grimly, "And don't take that winding path home, Steph. You're lucky to escape with only a few cuts."

The following day, as Stephanie was walking towards the school gate, she passed Chloe and her group of friends. She noted from the corner of her eye how Chloe's lips curled up slightly at one side.

"Where're you going, cry baby? How're your knees? Be careful where you go," sneered Chloe before bursting into laughter.

Stephanie could feel her face flush with embarrassment and her stomach clench. *Did they discover my hideout?*

As she started to feel herself overcome by fear and anxiety, she remembered her father's words. *She was loved. She wasn't alone.* She ignored their laughter and the tears that were gathering in her eyes, squared her shoulders, and walked ahead resolutely.

7
THE GOLD RING

A beautiful woman who has no sense
is like a gold ring in a pig's nose.
—Proverbs 11:22

"Phoebe, come for dinner," shouted Max.

"Tell Mum I'm not eating. I need to master these moves," said Phoebe.

"What moves?"

"Renegade. My friends have challenged me. Look how fast she is," said Phoebe referring to the dancer on the screen.

"She looks like a stick!" Max sneered, trying to imitate the moves.

"What do you know? I think she looks gorgeous!"

"Ay! What's this shiny thing on your finger? I've never seen it before. A *gold* ring? Who gave it to you?"

"Tsk, don't be so nosy! My friend gave it to me. It's just our group identity for the dance!"

Just then, Mum walked into the room.

"Phoebe, join us for dinner now," said Mum firmly.

Phoebe sat at the table sullenly and said, "Mum, I'm not hungry. I'll just eat the vegetables."

Her parents glanced at each other, but didn't try to change her mind.

After dinner, the Tan family came together for their nightly devotion.

Dad began, "There was a rich farmer whose proudest possession was his pig. He believed it brought him great wealth and protection. When bandits sneaked into the farm to steal his crops, the pig would alert the farmer by grunting really loudly. And whenever the farmer brought the pig with him to sell his crops, he was always able to obtain a handsome profit.

"The farmer cherished the pig so much that he made a bed for it in his room and allowed it to eat from the same table as him. Finally, one day, he even brought the pig to a goldsmith to fit a gold ring on the pig's nose."

"That's so silly," laughed Rick.

"What a waste, a gold ring on a pig's nose," said Phoebe.

"Well, Proverbs 11:22 says: '*A beautiful woman who has no sense is like a gold ring in a pig's nose.*' Yesterday, I visited a colleague's daughter in the hospital. She is 13 years old, but weighs only 20 kg now. She lost 25 kg over the past two months, and got so weak that she fainted. I didn't recognise her at first. She used to be rather charming."

"What happened to her?" Stephanie asked.

"She was diagnosed with anorexia, an eating disorder. For over two months, she had wanted to stay as thin as possible. She lost interest in food. When her mother forced her to eat, she would take as long as an hour to swallow just a spoonful of food," Dad explained.

"Why did she do that?" asked Rick.

"A boy she liked called her fat," Dad replied.

Mum turned to Phoebe and said, "Phoebe, we aren't stopping you from dancing, but dancing well doesn't mean you have to look like the girls in the challenge."

"Yeah, those girls look ridiculous in their oversized clothes," said Max.

"The gold ring, though valuable, loses its charm on the pig, just as a beautiful girl becomes less attractive when she acts without sense," said Mum.

Phoebe sat quietly, toying with the gold ring on her finger. Finally, she said sheepishly, "I think I'm feeling rather hungry now. Can we go for supper?"

"Sure. How about McDonald's?" asked Dad playfully.

"Okay," said Phoebe, shrugging her shoulders.

"Hurray!" Rick and Stephanie whooped together.

8
BODY AND BONES

A peaceful heart gives life to the body.
But jealousy rots the bones.
—Proverbs 14:30

One evening, the doorbell rang. It was Jannah and her mum.

"We came to thank you for the dress. Here are some muffins that we baked for your family," said Mrs Lim, smiling.

"You're most welcome! We hope the dress fits Jannah well," Mum said.

"It does, thank you again!" Mrs Lim said.

After Jannah and Mrs Lim left, Phoebe cried, "Mum! I asked for a dress last week to wear at Clara's birthday party, and you said no! Now you bought a dress for Jannah, who isn't even part of our family!"

"Phoebe, Mum and I found out that Mrs Lim needed to buy a dress for Jannah for her dance performance next week. Mrs Lim lost her job recently, and can't afford to buy one for her," Dad explained calmly.

"And after Mr Lim passed away, their family has been struggling to make ends meet. They've been such good friends to us for so long, dear, we had to help them," Mum explained.

Max blurted, "And, erm, how many dresses do you have now? Like… twenty?"

"Stop! It's just so unfair! I always have to give in to my siblings, and now I even have to give in to a stranger. Ya, ya, ya, I'm the eldest so I have to give in to everyone," Phoebe cried before running to her room and slamming the door.

A few minutes later, her parents knocked on her door and let themselves in, sitting on either side of their sobbing daughter.

"You're right, Phoebe, it isn't fair," Dad said quietly. Phoebe looked up at him, surprised. "A gift is never really 'fair', because it's giving someone something they didn't earn. When your mum and I give you kids gifts, it's not because you all have worked for it. It's because we love you, and want to do something special for you."

"It's the same for Jannah. We wanted to give her something special because she's going through a difficult time at home. It isn't fair either that she's lost her dad, and that her mum has lost her job. We wanted to show her that God loves her and has ways to provide for her needs, even though her father isn't around anymore."

Phoebe hiccupped as she tried to stop sobbing, "I know . . . but, it's just . . . if you give things to other people . . . doesn't it mean that you'll have less to give me?"

Mum moved to hug her daughter, "You know that's not true, dear. Yes, sometimes we might not have enough money to buy you everything you *want*, but we'll always do what we can to give you what you need."

"Last week, Rick received a new pair of soccer shoes because he's outgrown his," Dad said. "But Max will have to wait for his turn for those Nikes I know he's eyeing, because his shoes still fit. But it doesn't mean we love Max less than Rick. Just because we've given Jannah something that she needs now doesn't mean we've forgotten you, Phoebe. There's no need to be jealous."

Phoebe leaned against her mother, tear-streaked but thoughtful.

Dad continued, "Remember the verse we memorised last week? Proverbs 14:30 says: '*A peaceful heart gives life to the body. But jealousy rots the bones.*' Jealousy makes you look at what you don't have, instead of what you do have."

"If it controls you, you can't have peace in your heart, and you won't be able to enjoy the things and people in life," Mum added.

"I'm . . . I'm sorry, Mum and Dad," Phoebe mumbled. "You're right. I have many dresses and I don't need another one. Jannah needs one, not me."

Her parents looked at each other and smiled.

"Phoebe, actually, the reason your dad and I said no to buying you another dress was because we used the money to get something else for you," Mum said, handing Phoebe a box. "Something you need more . . ."

"Dancing shoes!" Phoebe exclaimed. "Does this mean I can join the hip-hop dance competition?" She had been talking about this event for months.

Her parents smiled and nodded.

"Thank you, Mum and Dad!" Phoebe said, throwing her arms around them.

9
SHOW-AND-TELL

The words of thoughtless people cut like swords.
But the tongue of wise people brings healing.
—Proverbs 12:18

Phoebe came rushing into the living room shouting, "Mum! Look what I found!"

She had been looking for some special paper in her mother's study for a secret project that her parents had entrusted to her, and found a yellowing postcard. "Is this you?"

Her mother looked up from the TV programme she was watching with Max and Stephanie, and glanced at the black-and-white drawing of herself as a young girl. "I forgot about that! Yes, a friend drew my portrait during recess once."

Rick walked in and looked over Phoebe's shoulder. "'Thank you for encouraging me. I want to be an artist one day'," he read. "What did you say to your friend, Mum?"

"Well, he was bullied quite a bit in school. His family was poor, and his mum would place a bowl on his head to trim his hair. You can imagine how much teasing he had to endure," said Mum. The poor guy would skip school a lot, or claim to have a stomachache and ask to go to the nurse.

"But I saw him drawing one day, and told him he was very talented. So he drew my portrait for me that afternoon. But he left the school eventually, too broken by all the nasty words," Mum sighed. "It's true what the Bible says: '*The words of thoughtless people cut like swords. But the tongue of wise people brings healing.*'"

"Do you know what happened to him, Mum?" Phoebe asked.

"The last I heard, he has become a rather successful photographer, famous for his black-and-white pictures."

"Maybe your words healed him!" Max exclaimed.

"Well, I sure hope they helped him in some way. Words are very powerful. They can make or break a person . . ."

That evening, after dinner, Mum gathered everyone. "Stephanie, we have a letter for you. Phoebe?"

Phoebe nodded, and took a letter out from her folder that she'd been working on in the afternoon. She read:

Dear Stephanie,

*You are helpful. You always volunteer to do the chores
for the family.*
You are smart. You are the best student among us.
*You are diligent. You always complete all your
homework before deadlines.*
*You are generous. You always share your birthday and
Christmas gifts with us.*
*You are creative. You always have a different way of
solving a problem.*
You are very dear to us, and we love you.

Love, Dad, Mum, Phoebe, Max, and Rick

Tears welled up in Stephanie's eyes as she heard the words from her family. "Thank you everyone," she said thickly. "It's . . . it's just that those words they said . . . still hurt very much. And I am really afraid of speaking in front of the class."

"Well, my offer still stands. Kong Fu Master Max at your service," Max said with a smile.

Stephanie laughed, and gently pushed Max.

"Well, Steph, we can't erase those hurtful words, but we *can* help you be ready for the next show-and-tell," said Dad.

The following week, the Tan family came together every evening to help Stephanie prepare for her show-and-tell. She had to speak about a family trip. After much debate, they finally decided on sharing about a holiday to Bintan.

Stephanie wrote the speech, and Mum edited it. Her dad and siblings looked for photographs and props. Everyone offered suggestions on how she could improve her presentation.

The day finally arrived. Everyone was quite excited to hear about each other's family trips. Sam spoke about his family trip to Hong Kong. Joelle shared about hers in Japan. Damien shared about his in Taiwan.

Stephanie watched nervously as Chloe delivered her flawless presentation about travelling to Paris with her family. The photographs of the Parisian sights were amazing. When she ended, she smirked at Stephanie and dropped a note on her desk. *Pale face, is yours about a trip to the zoo?*

Stephanie could feel the clenching pain in her stomach again. But instead of dwelling on it, she quickly read the letter that her family wrote to her. She was loved. She wasn't alone. Then, when it was her turn, Stephanie got up in front of her class, took a deep breath, and started her show-and-tell.

To everyone's astonishment, Stephanie's speech was moving, candid, and clear.

Her teacher was impressed and praised her, "You're right, Stephanie, we don't have to travel far to create beautiful memories. It's the people who travel with us that make a trip special. Well done!"

Making her way back to her seat, Stephanie could feel Chloe's cold stare following her. Strangely, Stephanie thought she saw sadness in those eyes. Dismissing Chloe, she soon noticed that there was no pain in her stomach anymore. Instead, she felt light and joyful.

The words of the wise have really brought healing to me, thought Stephanie.

10
VINEGAR AND SMOKE

Those who don't want to work hurt those who send them.
They are like vinegar on the teeth or smoke in the eyes.
—Proverbs 10:26

Rick, Max, Phoebe, and Stephanie sat at the dining table, eyeing the pile of potatoes and the huge bowl of quail eggs. They were tasked with preparing salad for a farewell party that evening. Uncle Albert and his family were emigrating to Australia.

"Must we spend our Saturday morning doing this?" Rick grumbled.

"I want to do other things too, but let's work together to finish this quickly," Phoebe suggested.

"Like dancing?" Max sneered while swirling one hand dramatically around his head. Phoebe glared at him and kicked his leg.

"Come on, let's get started," Stephanie said, trying to sound perky, "See, I have a lot in my bowl now."

"Why must we have a party? I hate these shells that stick to my fingers," Max whined.

Mum overheard their complaining, and shouted from the kitchen, "Kids, what was the verse we read this morning about vinegar and smoke?"

"'*Those who don't want to work hurt those who send them. They are like vinegar on the teeth or smoke in the eyes*'," Phoebe recited perfectly, while she flicked some eggshell off her fingers.

"Yes. Try not to be too tedious to my teeth and eyes, please!"

"Sluggards," Phoebe shout-whispered at the boys.

"You, too!" Rick hissed back.

"HEY!" Mum yelled again.

"Sorry, Mum!" they chorused, and got back to work.

That evening, the Tan family drove to Uncle Albert's apartment. Much to Max's dismay, he had the unpleasant task of starting the fire at the barbecue pit with Dad. The smoke stung his eyes. He coughed and winced as he stared miserably at the huge pile of food to be cooked.

Max was tasked to barbecue the food with his cousin, Tim.

"Max and Tim, join us for water polo!" John, Tim's brother, shouted from the pool.

At that moment, an idea struck Max. He and Tim emptied a container of meat and two packets of sausages. They arranged the food on the grill hastily and ran to the pool.

After scoring a few rounds in the game, Max suddenly remembered the food on the grill. He raced towards the pit, but the smell of burnt meat greeted him even before he saw the shrivelled pieces of meat and sausages.

Max was horrified. Just as he was wondering how to salvage their dinner, Dad and Uncle Albert walked over. Max apologised, and watched as they threw away the charred food.

"Don't worry, I'll barbecue the rest," Uncle Albert said, smiling reassuringly at Max.

Flushed with guilt and shame, Max stood at the pit with Uncle Albert for the rest of the evening to cook the remaining food. But he could barely enjoy his dinner, with the waste caused by his actions leaving a bad taste in his mouth.

Over breakfast the next morning, Max said in remorse, "Mum, I'm sorry for ruining the dinner you prepared yesterday. Dad, I'm sorry I was so irresponsible. I think I understand why sluggards are like vinegar to the teeth and smoke to the eyes. They're unpleasant and irritating, because their laziness messes things up for no good reason."

"Yeah," Rick added, "Mum, I'm sorry I was unwilling to help with the food preparation yesterday. I didn't make it any easier for you."

"Thanks, kids," Mum said, smiling at them. Dad patted Max on his shoulder, "It's alright, son. I'm glad you've understood why it's important to be diligent about your tasks. I know Uncle Albert appreciated your help afterwards."

"I shouldn't have complained about the prep too. I will help to wipe the table later," Rick chimed in.

"I will wash the dishes," volunteered Phoebe.

"I'll dry them," said Stephanie.

"And I will help to eat," said Max.

Everyone cackled with laugher.

From **Emma Lin** to **Me**: (Privately)
hi
hi

From **Me** to **Emma Lin**: (Privately)
hi

From **Emma Lin** to **Me**: (Privately)
Nice background

From **Me** to **Emma Lin**: (Privately)
Thanks

From **Emma Lin** to **Me**: (Privately)
What school are you in? Mine is CHIJ Katong

From **Me** to **Emma Lin**: (Privately)
St Andrew's Junior

From **Emma Lin** to **Me**: (Privately)
Nice

From **Emma Lin** to **Me**: (Privately)
I like dogs

From **Me** to **Emma Lin**: (Privately)
I am fine with them

From **Emma Lin** to **Me**: (Privately)
hehe

From **Emma Lin** to **Me**: (Privately)
Er . . . I wanted to tell you this a long time ago
But I was scared. Now here
Like you
I like you

From **Me** to **Emma Lin**: (Privately)
Oh ok ☺

Send to: Everyone

Tap here to chat or tap a message to reply

11
DO YOU LIKE DOGS?

Think carefully about the paths that your feet walk on.
Always choose the right ways.
—Proverbs 4:26

"Owww . . . Max has an admirer. So, you were busy chatting with a girl during online tuition class," teased Phoebe.

Max retorted, "No, I was paying attention all the time. Today's passage is about a lost dog, and the teacher was explaining the passage to us when Emma started chatting with me."

Mum asked, "How did you feel about being noticed?"

"Hmm, good actually," replied Max honestly.

"What do you think you should do next?" Dad asked.

"Well, I guess . . . we'll be friends," said Max.

"Ewww, Max has a girlfriend! Some of my friends also have girlfriends," exclaimed Rick excitedly.

"Kids, have a look at Proverbs 4:26: '*Think carefully about the paths that your feet walk on. Always choose the right ways*'," said Dad. When I was slightly older than Max, I once gave this girl the impression that I liked her. My classmate, Wendy, was struggling with her subjects, so I helped her with her homework. To thank me, she wrote me letters and bought me gifts. She even waited to walk home with me every day.

"I just went along with it, thinking I was just being friendly. I didn't realise she had a crush on me until a very wise girl told me about it." Dad smiled and winked at Mum.

"Anyway, after I found out, I realised it wasn't right to give her the wrong impression. So when Wendy waited for me at the school gate, I told her I was going to take a different path home. She looked puzzled and embarrassed at first. But after a few weeks, she realised I was not interested in her, and avoided me after that. I knew she was hurt, but it was better that she knew the truth than to let her keep thinking I liked her too. I have this very wise girl to thank," said Dad, reaching out to hold Mum's hand.

"Oooh, Mum was the wise girl you fell in love with!" exclaimed Stephanie.

"Yes," chuckled Dad as he looked at Mum lovingly, "'*Who can find an excellent woman? She is worth far more than rubies.*'"

"Awww . . . that's so sweet," chorused the children.

"Hehe . . . I was quoting Proverbs 31:10," Dad said. "Anyhow, I hope you will choose your paths carefully. Unless you've found someone more precious than rubies, don't do anything to let them think you're interested. Taking the wrong paths will bring you, and others, pain later."

"Okay, Dad," said Max.

"So, do you still like dogs?" asked Rick cheekily.

Max sprang on Rick, and the two started wrestling on the floor in a playful brawl.

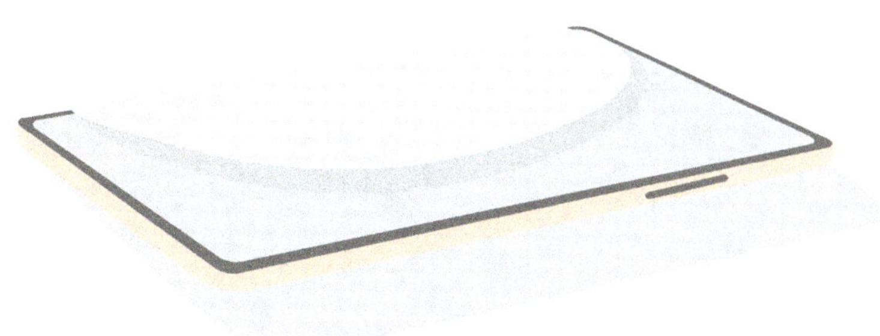

12

SMASHED

Anyone who is patient has great understanding.
But anyone who gets angry quickly shows how foolish they are.
—Proverbs 14:29

Max exclaimed, "Mum, Jayden was punched today! There was a lot of blood!"

"Oh dear. What happened?" Mum asked as she gave him his afternoon snack.

"We were walking to our classroom after assembly, and Jayden kept teasing Wei Liang about his new haircut," Max said in between bites. "Wei Liang was so furious, he smacked Jayden's face really hard. Jayden's face swelled up, and there was blood everywhere. He didn't lose any teeth, though."

"Oh, poor Jayden! He shouldn't have teased Wei Liang, but Wei Liang shouldn't have hit him like that too!"

"Yes, we were all shocked. Wei Liang was sent to the principal, and his parents were called. I heard he will have detention for one full week."

"Well, anger can make us behave foolishly sometimes. Remember Proverbs 14:29? *'Anyone who is patient has great understanding . . .'"*

"'. . . but anyone who gets angry quickly shows how foolish they are'," continued Max as he ate the last of his *kueh*. "Hey Mum, can I meet Jake and the others later at 4 p.m. to play *Among Us?*"

"Alright, but finish your homework first," replied Mum.

"Of course."

It was 3 p.m.

Max was playing with Rick.

"Max, watch your time. Aren't you going to do your homework?" asked Mum.

"Wait!"

3:30 p.m.

Max finally started doing his homework.

3:55 p.m.

"Mum, can I do my homework later? I'm meeting Jake soon!"

"No, Max. You said you'd complete it."

"Arrrh! But it's almost time," cried Max and banged his fist on the table several times. He hurried to finish his homework.

4:15 p.m.

"Arr . . . why's the screen blank? Mum, the laptop's not working! What's happening? I need to meet my friends online! Mum, help!" Max shouted anxiously.

"Wait, I'm preparing dinner."

"But I'm late. You've to help me now!"

"Stop yelling, Max. Use the iPad first," Mum said, handing it to him. She sighed as she looked at the blank screen. "The laptop's new. Your Dad's going to be so upset."

Later that day, Mum asked Max, "What happened exactly? Was the screen blank from the start, or only after you logged in?

Max hesitated. "Well, I . . . I . . . punched the keyboard with my fist," he finally confessed. "But it was because I waited for a long while and the screen didn't come on. Plus, I was already late for the game!"

"You vented your anger on the laptop because you were late for a game? Dad *just* bought the laptop. Now, we'll have to borrow another laptop from someone so you can still attend your online lessons, while we send this laptop for repair. Your actions affect other people, Max!"

"Sorry, Mum," Max mumbled, hanging his head.

"Do you remember what Proverbs 14:29 says about anger?"

After a long pause, Max replied, "I was quick to anger and behaved foolishly. I had behaved just like Wei Liang. Sorry."

"Why were you angry in the first place?"

"'Er . . . because I was late for the game."

"And why were you late?"

"I delayed doing my homework."

"Yes. If you'd completed your homework earlier, you wouldn't be late for your game. And if you weren't late, you wouldn't be so angry. So, to avoid this next time, don't procrastinate."

"Sorry, Mum. I'll apologise to Dad later."

13
ADDICTION

People are wise and understanding
when they think about the way they live.
But people are foolish when their foolish ways trick them.
—Proverbs 14:8

Click click click click click click click click click click click
Max furiously clicked away at the trackpad. Each click got him a point that brought him closer to getting a Brawler. He had been clicking for nearly an hour, and had collected five Brawlers.

But Mum's booming voice jolted him from his concentration. "Didn't you say 15 minutes more? It's been an hour!"

"Yes, yes, yes, 10 more minutes."

"And what's this intriguing game you're playing?" Mum asked, walking into the room.

"I am collecting Brawlers. I need to collect all. If I stop the game, I'll lose all the Brawlers I've collected so far," Max explained, pointing at the side of the screen to show her what he had already collected, rapidly clicking away the whole time.

"And how do you get these Brawlers?"

"Just click to get the scores. A thousand clicks for a Brawler."

"And how many Brawlers do you want to collect?"

"All twenty."

"A thousand clicks for a Brawler. That means 20,000 clicks! And that means at least six hours of non-stop clicking! Are you training for finger fencing?" teased Phoebe, who was listening to the conversation.

Max glanced at Phoebe and stuck his tongue out at her.

"Do you find this fun? Just clicking away?" Mum asked, trying to conceal her surprise.

Max admitted sheepishly, "Erm, well, it's not *that* fun, but if I collect all the Brawlers, I'll be happy. I wouldn't mind doing this the whole day."

"Be careful what you ask for," Mum warned and walked away.

The following day, the Tan family was learning to play a new card game, The Lord of the Rings. They read through the character cards, and Mum flashed the card she was holding in her hand. "Kids, remember Gandalf?"

"He was the wise wizard," replied Stephanie.

"Yes. In the story, he wisely chose not to take the ring, because he was afraid the ring's power would become too addictive for him. And he knew that the ring's power would ultimately enslave and corrupt him, so he stayed away from it," said Mum.

"This reminds me of a verse I read this morning in Proverbs 14:8: *'People are wise and understanding when they think about the way they live. But people are foolish when their foolish ways trick them'*," Dad chimed in.

He continued, "Gandalf wisely knew that the ring would eventually enslave him, so he resisted the temptation and fled from it. But other foolish characters were deceived into thinking that they were stronger than the ring. They tried to possess it and use its power, but ended up being destroyed instead."

"What is the 'ring' in your life now, kids? Are you fleeing from it, or are you allowing it to trick you?" Mum added.

There was a moment of silence as everyone thought about the questions.

"I know. Max's ring is his computer games!" Rick replied.

Max retorted with frustration, "Shut up! I like playing games. It's fun. And I don't see why I'm not allowed to play as much as I want after I've finished my schoolwork. My classmates are allowed to play at least two to three hours a day! I'm only allowed an hour each week! How's that a lot? It's not my 'ring'. IT ISN'T CONTROLLING ME!"

"Max, calm down, and please don't yell at your brother," Mum said firmly.

Dad asked gently, "Max, what do you think are the signs of game addiction?"

Max bit his lip and crossed his arms, looking defiant yet trying not to cry. "I don't know."

Dad nodded, acknowledging his answer. "What do the rest of you think?" he asked, addressing the other children.

"Well . . ." Stephanie piped up nervously, "When you can't stop . . ."

"And when you get angry about not being allowed to play," Rick added. "Last week, Max got angry and smashed the laptop when he couldn't play with his friends on time—"

"—NO! I was angry because I was late!" cried Max.

"Max, stop yelling," said Mum, giving his hand a tight squeeze.

Dad said gently, "I can see that you're upset, Max. What are you feeling?"

Max started sobbing, "Well, maybe I . . . I'm . . . slightly addicted to gaming. I can't stop thinking about the games I play, and always want to play more. It makes me mad whenever Mum asks me to stop, and doesn't give me more time . . . but I don't know how to change!"

Dad put his arm around Max's shoulder. "Well, one of the ways to stop an addiction from getting worse is to take a break from it. For about three weeks. That's usually the amount of time it takes to form a new habit. What do you think?"

"I can try . . ." Max replied sadly.

"That's a wise decision, son. Dad and I are not trying to stop you from having fun, but when gaming turns addictive, it can bring harm to you and others," Mum said.

"And besides fasting from computer games, you'll need to fill your time with other activities. Shall we go on a hike this weekend? Let's go to a park that we haven't explored," Dad suggested.

"How about a game of football, too?" Max asked.

"Sure, son," Dad said, ruffling Max's hair and giving him a bear hug.

14
PHONE

Start children off on the right path.
And even when they are old, they will not turn away from it.
—Proverbs 22:6

It was a Sunday afternoon, and the Tan family was happily slurping bubble tea that Dad bought.

"Mum and Dad, when can I have a phone? Most of my friends have their own phones and I feel so left out," Max lamented. "We had to discuss a project last week, and my group communicated over the phone. They could only update me when they saw me in class."

"Max, Mum and I feel that you're still not ready to own a phone. You'll have to wait," Dad answered.

"How long must I wait? I've been memorising verses, and I think I'm pretty wise now," Max said, feeling disappointed.

"We know it's not easy to be different from others, son. You may have to find other ways to communicate with your friends. At this moment, we feel that you might need to learn to exercise greater self-control over your screen time. We're also hoping to see you being more responsible in handling the tasks and chores entrusted to you," Mum explained.

"How about me? When can I get mine?" asked Phoebe.

Mum and Dad exchanged looks. "Phoebe, Mum and I have discussed and we think you're ready to own a phone," Dad smiled.

Phoebe's eyes grew wide, "You mean now?"

"Yes!" Dad replied.

"What! She gets to have hers? That's unfair," Max said sullenly.

Dad explained, "Max, you see, Mum and I have the responsibility to do what Proverbs 22:6 says, that is: '*Start children off on the right path. And even when they are old, they will not turn away from it*'. We need to give you freedom and responsibility at the right time, so that all of you will continue to do what is right even as you grow older.

"Mum and I have observed that Phoebe has become more responsible, doing her chores without grumbling. She has also exercised greater self-control over her screen time recently. Last Sunday, she led the worship during Sunday school, and the teachers praised her for being responsible and willing to learn."

Mum added, "I've also observed that Phoebe has consistently returned the phone to me after her time on TikTok, without me having to remind her."

"She's also no longer just eating vegetables, too, and is putting on weight," Rick chipped in cheekily.

Phoebe elbowed Rick playfully.

"But the phone doesn't come without strings attached," Mum said. "You'll need to agree to some conditions, Phoebe."

She laid out a piece of paper on the dining table, and the children gathered around it in earnest.

"Wow! There are fifteen rules in this contract!" Rick cried.

"I agree that if I am unable to keep up with my household, church, and financial responsibilities, or if I demonstrate untrustworthy behaviour, my phone will be taken away . . ." read Stephanie.

"Are you going to sign this?" Rick asked, as everyone looked at Phoebe.

Phoebe remained silent as she stared at each term on the contract.

"Phoebe, we love you. We want you to see that owning a phone is a privilege as well as a responsibility," Dad explained. "You'll have the freedom to decide how you will use this phone, but only if you follow the rules we've set for you. And you'll need to continue to show us you're trustworthy in order to enjoy this privilege of using it. Ultimately, the contract is to protect you, not restrict you."

Phoebe took a deep breath and nodded. "Dad and Mum, I know you love me. I'll do my best to abide by these rules. My siblings are my witnesses. They can remind me if I forget." Reaching across the table for the pen, she signed the contract.

"Well, then," Dad said, smiling as he handed her a glossy box, "Here's your new phone."

"Aww," Max's heart swelled with envy as he watched Phoebe open her gift. Turning to his parents, he said with great determination, "I'll prove to you I can be responsible to handle a phone, too!"

Dad chuckled, "Yes, I believe in you, son."

CONTRACT

ALDEN
18

RICK
27

15
MR POPULAR

A person with unfaithful friends soon comes to ruin.
But there is a friend who sticks closer than a brother.
—Proverbs 18:24

Rick strode across the road to get to the bus stop, furiously wiping his eyes. When he finally saw his mother, he fell into her arms, crying uncontrollably.

"What happened?" Mum asked worriedly as she held him. Stephanie, who was dismissed from school earlier, stood beside Mum and placed her hand on Rick's quivering shoulders.

"Just now, we had to write a card to thank someone in the class. I wrote to Zack . . . but h-h-he took one look at my card . . . and tore . . . i-i-t," Rick stuttered miserably. "Mum, I treat him as my best friend but he . . . he has so many friends. He doesn't need me."

"It must have hurt a lot to see your card being torn. That wasn't kind of Zack. Perhaps you could tell him how you feel about this? Meanwhile, there are other friends in your class. Maybe you could get to know them better," Mum suggested.

"I've tried to be kind to everyone! But nobody gave me a card. I wish I could be as popular as Zack. He gets invited to every birthday party. Today, Gerald invited some friends to the sea aquarium for his birthday party! But I didn't get an invitation," Rick sighed.

"It's not so bad, son. You do have good friends, too. What about Alden? He invited you to his party last month, remember?"

"Yes, at least you have Alden," mumbled Stephanie, lost in her thoughts.

"But that's just *one* friend. I want *more* friends. . ." Rick grumbled, slumping onto the seat at the bus stop.

"Rick, there's a saying in the Bible: '*A person with unfaithful friends soon comes to ruin. But there is a friend who sticks closer than a brother.*' It's not about how many friends you have. You just need *one* friend who is good to you!" Mum said, patting his arm.

"Well, at least I can still join Zack's football team tomorrow as goalkeeper," said Rick, perking up.

The following day, Rick was playing football at the school field with Alden, Zack, and his friends. They were playing against several older boys who were known for playing rough.

"Let's trash them today. I hate the way they smirk. They've no skills, only sneaky tricks," Zack sneered, determined to defeat them. But Rick quivered, as the opponents appeared stronger and bigger.

After 15 minutes, the opponents were leading 3-1.

"Hey Rick, can you focus? If you let the opponent in one more time, you are out of the team!" Zack yelled. Poor Rick. He was stiff with fear, making him less alert and agile than usual.

Immediately after the half-time break, Alden scored a goal for their team. But unfortunately, as the game was about to end, the ball whizzed past Rick again and into the goal. The game ended with the opponents winning 4-2.

"You are so hopeless! That was the third ball you missed! Stay away from my team next time," yelled Zack, storming off with his friends.

Rick slumped to the ground and cried.

"It wasn't your fault that we lost the game today. Zack missed the chance to score when he was given a free kick. He was just angry about his mistake but refused to admit it," Alden said.

"I won't be able to join his team in future. I've wanted so much to be his good friend," said Rick, sobbing quietly.

"Don't worry, we can form our own team. Let's go. I'll buy you ice-cream," Alden said to Rick with a bright smile.

There is indeed a friend who sticks closer than a brother, thought Rick, as he grabbed Alden's hand and stood up. The two friends left the school field happily, chattering excitedly about their holiday plans.

16
A DREAM COME TRUE

An honest witness saves lives.
But a dishonest witness tells lies.
—Proverbs 14:25

"Christopher and some boys just kept calling him names—loser, dumb, stupid. And Khairul just sat there. But when they called him 'black boy', Khairul got really mad. He got up from his seat and shoved his desk so hard that it hit Christopher. Christopher lost his balance and fell . . ."

Rick stopped dramatically, keeping his family in suspense as he recounted the incident that had happened in class that day.

"Then, Mr Chia, our discipline master, came in and saw Christopher on the floor. Christopher pretended to groan loudly and accused Khairul of starting the fight. His gang also started saying that it was Khairul's fault. Then the rest of the class joined in to say, 'Khairul started it! Khairul started it!' Even the class monitor! But Khairul kept insisting it wasn't his fault."

"And did *you* join in, son?" Dad asked, winking at Rick, already guessing how the story was going to end.

"No! I stood up and told Mr Chia about the name-calling. He was so mad. He scolded Christopher and his friends, and even called their parents!" Rick ended with a proud smile.

"Rick, you're a hero!" said Stephanie.

"You did the right thing by telling the truth, Rick. '*An honest witness saves lives. But a dishonest witness tells lies.*' You saved Khairul from being unfairly punished," said Dad.

"Yes, I'm glad you stood up for him. He must have felt terrible when everyone turned on him. All that name-calling is unacceptable," said Mum.

"I feel sad for him. He doesn't have many friends . . . Mum, I don't understand why Christopher and his gang pick on Khairul. Is it because he's got dark skin?" Rick asked, finally voicing out a question that he'd been struggling with for a while. "What's the big deal?"

"It shouldn't be a big deal, Rick, you're right," Mum said, relieved that her son had some good sense. "But some people make judgments about others based on foolish reasons. They wrongly assume that just because someone has a certain skin colour, they also have certain character traits. That's completely wrong. A person's skin colour doesn't determine who they are. It's who they are on the inside that counts."

"Yeah . . . and Khairul is really nice. He helped me with my math problem after class the other day when I couldn't understand what Ms Lin was saying. Maybe I can ask him to hang out with Alden and me during recess."

"That's a good idea," said Dad approvingly.

Two days later, Rick came home, bubbly and cheerful. He showed Mum a hand-made card that Khairul had left on his desk:

Dear Rick,

Thank you for standing up for me and sitting with me during recess. I would like to invite you to my birthday party at Resorts World Sentosa S.E.A. Aquarium next Saturday. I hope you can come.

Khairul

"Mum, I can't believe this! The aquarium! It's my dream come true," exclaimed Rick.

"It sure is," said Mum, giving Rick a tight hug.

SEE NO EVIL

Wise people see danger and go to a safe place.
But childish people keep going and suffer for it.
—Proverbs 22:3

Max and his classmates hurried towards the computer lab. Lessons at the lab were always something to look forward to, as it meant an hour away from the sun-baked classroom—and an opportunity to sneak into gaming sites while the teacher was not looking. Max took his seat beside Ryan and logged into their Google Classroom as their maths teacher, Ms Shereen, gave instructions for the assignments that afternoon.

Midway through the lesson, Max was having trouble playing a video. As he turned to Ryan for help, Max caught a glimpse of something on his friend's screen, and immediately turned away.

"Ryan, what're you doing?" Max exclaimed, keeping his eyes averted from Ryan's screen.

"What's wrong? My dad looks at these pictures, too," sneered Ryan.

But Max knew it wasn't right to look at them. He got up immediately and informed Ms Shereen. By the time she walked to Ryan, he was doing his maths assignment and denied having gone to other websites. But Ms Shereen did a quick check on the web browser's history log, and told Ryan that she would be informing his parents. After Ms Shereen walked away, Ryan gave Max the middle finger, and threatened to get back at him.

That night, Dad was telling Mum about an incident that he witnessed. "I saw a mother telling her son to tie up his shoelaces at the train station this afternoon. But he just made a face at her, and scooted off down the escalator. Half a minute later, we both heard a sharp cry, and saw the boy sprawling at the bottom of the escalator. He'd fallen because his laces got caught in it!"

Mum winced. "That silly kid. I hope he wasn't too badly hurt?"

"He was alright. I hit the emergency button to stop the escalator so his mother could yank his shoelaces out. Hopefully, he'll learn to listen next time," Dad said. Noticing that Max was listening to their conversation, Dad winked at him and said, "It's like I always say, son, '*Wise people see danger and go to a safe place. But childish people keep going and suffer for it'*."

"That's from Proverbs, right?" Max mumbled.

"Mm-hmm. When we keep going in the direction of danger, we'll suffer the consequences. Just like the boy did."

"Dad, I . . . I saw something dangerous today," said Max.

Both his parents turned to him. "What was it?" Dad asked.

"I shouldn't say. It was very bad," Max mumbled, shaking his head.

There was a moment of silence as his parents waited for Max to speak.

"Girls without clothes. But I turned away immediately. Ms Shereen brought us to the computer lab for our maths lesson, and Ryan was looking at those pictures," Max confessed.

Dad and Mum glanced at each other. "You did the right thing, son," Mum said, "Did you tell Ms Shereen?"

"Yes, I did. You've both warned me before about such pictures. I knew they weren't good for me, so I didn't look at them," said Max.

"I'm glad you told us, son," Dad said, "Those images can stick in your memory for a long time, and tempt you to sin. But more importantly, they're disrespectful to women."

"Turning away early will keep you from suffering later," Mum chimed in. "You did well today, Max."

18
REVELATION

A person who is a false witness against a neighbor
is like a club, a sword or a sharp arrow.
—Proverbs 25:18

Chik . . . chik . . . chik . . .

The room was dim except for the last ray of the evening sun filtering through the flapping blinds, casting a fuzzy reflection on the shiny blade.

Chik . . . chik . . . chik . . .

The blade dived repeatedly at the wooden desk, creating a small hole. In the background, "The Muffin Song" was playing softly: the muffin was inviting others to eat him so that he could die, die, die.

Stephanie tasted the salt from her tears as she placed the blade on her wrist and made slow circling movements on her skin. She pressed the blade lightly before pausing, wiping away her tears, and breaking down in heavy sobs again.

Ding, ding, ding, ding. A slew of messages came in on her phone. Stephanie read them and her eyes widened in horror. Chloe had posted numerous messages on their class chat group, calling Stephanie a string of hateful names. She was horrified to see a video of her falling in the field after she was startled by a grass snake, and a photograph of her crying in the school garden.

Messages came in fast and furious as her other classmates in the group commented:

"You are so ugly."

"Weak!"

"Too bad, James doesn't like a cry baby."

Chloe and her friends knew she had a crush on James, and had been taunting her ever since they found out. Now everyone in class would know, too. Distraught and crushed, Stephanie threw her phone on the floor and cried. Mum, who had heard Stephanie's scream, knocked on her door before opening it, to find her sobbing into her pillow.

The sobs grew louder as Mum approached and placed her hand gently on Stephanie.

"I wanna die, leave me alone. I'm the ugliest and the weakest. Nobody likes me!"

Mum paused the music that was still playing in the background.

"God loves you." After a long pause, Mum spoke again, "You aren't the ugliest. You aren't the weakest. And you do have some good friends—and your family loves you deeply."

Mum continued, "Listening to these lies will leave you broken. Sad songs with depressing lyrics will make you feel worse . . . "

Ding, ding, ding, ding. Messages continued to come in.

"Look at these messages! My reputation is ruined," Stephanie cried as she showed her mother the messages. "I hate Chloe. I hate school!"

Mum's face went white with rage as she read the messages.

"Now you understand? How can I possibly not be upset?" Stephanie cried.

Noticing the blade in Stephanie's hand, Mum gently pried it from her, only to discover fresh cuts on her hand.

Concern replaced the fury on her face. "You've hurt yourself!" Mum gasped.

In between sobs, Stephanie said, "Mum, cutting helps to relieve some pain. Each time I dig with my blade, I just think of hurting them for all the bad things they say about me."

"But you are hurting yourself instead." Mum's voice quavered slightly as she gently touched the wounds in disbelief. Regaining her composure, she began, "Yes, it is very difficult not to be upset and angry with them. I know they've hurt you deeply. Their cutting words hurt like *'a club, a sword or a sharp arrow'* (Proverbs 25:18)."

"But hurting yourself isn't going to help them understand the pain that they've inflicted on you. And thinking of ways to hurt others will only make you more miserable. What they say about you is certainly unacceptable. We'll need to speak to your teachers and inform Chloe's parents."

Stephanie nodded silently.

Removing the blade from Stephanie's hand, Mum continued, "Please promise me not to hurt yourself again. We love you, and God loves you too."

"Mum, please, I would like to be alone for a while."

"Alright, dear. We'll talk about this later. But remember you're not alone, okay?"

Just then, Phoebe entered the room and declared, "The world's best muffins have been born. Want to try some?"

Mum and Stephanie looked at each other. "It's muffin time," Stephanie said, managing a weak smile.

STEPHANIE

A cheerful heart makes you healthy.
But a broken spirit dries you up.
—Proverbs 17:22

"Thank you, Mrs Tan and Madam Teo, for coming here today," said Miss Tay, Stephanie's form teacher, as she began the meeting. "This is Mrs Raj, our school counsellor. Madam Teo has already been informed about Chloe's behaviour in class. We'd now like to explain what the school will be doing to help both Chloe and Stephanie."

"I don't know why Chloe is behaving this way," Madam Teo started a little defensively. "Maybe it's just a misunderstanding. Ever since I divorced Chloe's father, I've been very busy working. But I give her and her brother all they need. And I think I provide for them better than most families do. Last December, I even brought them to Paris. She's a very fortunate child. I don't think the problem lies with her."

"Madam Teo and Mrs Tan, usually, children bully for a reason," Mrs Raj explained gently. "When their parents divorce, kids might feel very vulnerable and insecure. Sometimes, their insecurity might be the reason why they bully others."

Mrs Raj continued: Chloe has shared with me that she is envious of how close Stephanie is to her family. After the show-and-tell in class two weeks ago, Chloe came to see me. She had wanted Stephanie to be jealous of her family trip to Paris. But when she heard Stephanie's presentation about how the love in her family made her own trip meaningful and enjoyable, Chloe felt devastated. This is something she misses in her own family.

"From what I gather, Chloe is struggling to cope with her pain of not having a complete family, and expresses it by bullying Stephanie. Her feelings are valid but her actions are, of course, unacceptable. We've spoken to her, and she understands that she has to be disciplined."

Madam Teo shrugged slightly, but remained silent and expressionless.

Stephanie's mum finally broke the uncomfortable silence. "Thank you, Mrs Raj, for explaining the situation. This has definitely helped me understand Chloe better. Both girls have been hurt deeply in different ways. Hopefully, with the school's help, the two girls can receive healing, and enjoy being in school again. I'll speak to Stephanie and do what I can to help her understand the situation."

That evening, Mum took Stephanie to a nearby park. They sat on a bench, and Mum told Stephanie about the meeting with Chloe's mother. Stephanie nodded, and gazed silently at a flock of pigeons jostling for some pieces of bread on the ground.

She noticed a rather scrawny pigeon pecking on a small piece of bread. Suddenly, a bigger but limping pigeon fluttered in and snatched it away. Stephanie uttered a helpless yelp.

After a while, Stephanie spoke. "Am I supposed to forgive her because she has a *valid* reason for being mean? She has hurt me deeply. I don't want to forgive her."

Standing up, Stephanie urged her mother to follow her. "Come, I'll show you something." They went down a winding, gravelly path that cut through some thick undergrowth and stopped in front of a trumpet tree.

She pointed at its trunk. "Mum, look at this. For a long time, every time the girls hurt me, I resisted the urge to hurt myself by digging at the tree. See how deep the cavity is? But their words started to hurt so much that I started to hurt myself to lessen the pain. I could pretend that it was them I was hurting for all the bad things they said about me. But . . . I still feel miserable."

"I can understand why you can't forgive her yet, but if you keep thinking about how much you hate Chloe and the other girls, it'll make you more miserable," Mum said sadly as she touched the gouge in the tree trunk. "All the hatred in your heart will make you feel sick. Remember your memory verse from Sunday school, Proverbs 17:22? It states that *'a cheerful heart makes you healthy'*."

"I tried to think about things that make me happy, but I can't stop thinking about the hurt they've brought me. Those hurtful words just keep coming back," Stephanie mumbled.

"It's not just about thinking about things that make you happy," Mum said gently. "It's also about letting go of your hurts. It's about forgiving those who've hurt you."

"I . . . I find it so difficult to forgive all of them."

"Yes, it *is* difficult," said Mum as she gave Stephanie a tight hug. "You know, forgiveness isn't about pretending that they've never hurt you. It's accepting that they are broken people who are equally hurt and helpless, and there's nothing they can do to take back the pain they've caused you.

"Forgiveness is letting go of needing to 'hurt them back' for the pain they've caused you, and letting God make you whole instead . . . broken people can't heal you, Steph, only God can."

Stephanie nodded silently.

Mum continued, "When you forgive, the anger and sadness will leave you. In time, as God heals you, you will feel joy again. I know you might not feel ready now, but we can pray that God will help you want to forgive Chloe."

"I don't wish to feel miserable. Mum, can you pray for me?"

"Of course. I'll be happy to."

20
REFLECTIONS

Respect for [or fear of] the Lord is like a fountain that gives life.
It turns you away from the jaws of death.
—Proverbs 14:27

"A cemetery? Why are we here?" Phoebe asked Dad as he parked the family car by the side of the road.

"Fun. I haven't been to one," Rick remarked.

"It's creepy," said Stephanie in a low voice.

"Follow me. I'd like you to visit someone," said Dad.

As they walked up an uneven footpath, the children examined the headstones. Some looked impressive with trim foliage and flowers, while others appeared neglected.

"Wow, look at this one!" Rick exclaimed excitedly, pointing to several remote-controlled cars that were neatly assembled in front of a headstone.

"And here's a huge Lego *Iron Man!* He must have been a great fan!" cried Max.

"And this one's surely a fan of *Pokémon*," said Rick, admiring the collection of *Pokémon* figurines. "Oh, he was only 11 years old—Max's age."

"This one has a collection of dolls. Oh . . . she was only six," added Stephanie grimly.

"The dead can't bring their collections with them, however large they are," Phoebe murmured thoughtfully.

The children examined each headstone curiously as they walked along. Finally, Dad stopped at Uncle Sim's headstone.

"Oh, Uncle Sim! I remember him. He loved nature. During a hiking trip, he taught me many things about plants and flowers," recalled Max.

Dad smiled, "That's right. It's Uncle Sim's death anniversary next week."

"He always had a kind word for me whenever I met him," said Stephanie.

"He gave time to people. I remember when Elizabeth and I were fighting once in Sunday school. Uncle Sim heard us and helped us work it out," said Phoebe.

"He died young," Max noted, sadly.

Dad nodded, "Yes. He lived a short but well-spent life. He loved God dearly, and that was what enabled him to love people around him."

"I don't want to die, at least not so young," said Max quietly.

"We'll all experience physical death, and there's no way we can determine the length of our stay here on earth," said Mum.

"He was a godly man. Why did God allow him to die so young?" Stephanie asked.

"Well, in a way, death did not end his life, because he impacted many lives. When Uncle Sim was alive, his life truly reflected what Proverbs 14:27 says: *'Respect for [or fear of] the* LORD *is like a fountain that gives life. It turns you away from the jaws of death'*. He chose to honour God in many ways, and many people have benefitted from his wise living," said Dad.

"He obeyed God by giving up a comfortable life and a promising career to be a missionary. Sometimes, choosing to fear God will involve making sacrifices, but it will help you walk wisely and keep you away from the consequences of wrong choices."

After a while, Dad asked, "Kids, what does fearing God look like to you?"

The children were quiet for a while as they thought about their father's question. Then, stopping in her tracks, Phoebe said, "I think fearing God means understanding that life doesn't revolve around my needs and wants, but doing what God would want. I think I used to be quite self-centred, and thought that something was fair only if it benefited me. But life is unfair for a lot of people, and maybe fearing God means that I give some of my things to them so that they can know His love for them. How does that sound, Dad?"

Dad's heart swelled with pride as he thought about how much his eldest daughter had grown in the last few months. "That sounds great, Phoebe. How about you Max?"

"Well, I certainly need to learn to control my anger. Fearing God means I honour Him by using my time wisely and respecting the limits on my screen time set by you and Mum. It also means fleeing from websites that are displeasing to God," Max replied. He ruffled Rick's hair playfully and said, "Your turn."

"Hmm . . . Fearing God is the best thing in life, because you get to go to the aquarium for free!" Rick exclaimed, drawing laughs from the rest. Clearing his throat in an exaggerated manner, he continued, "Fearing God is about defending the weak and less popular, because this is what Jesus would do. Fearing God is about being with friends who are wise, humble and kind, like my best friend, Alden."

There was a moment of silence as everyone waited for Stephanie to share. The Tan family came to a pavement that was littered with brown leaves and flowers. Stephanie stopped and looked up. It was a trumpet tree in full bloom. She rested her hands on the sturdy trunk, and her fingers gently traced the jagged lines on the tree bark.

"Fearing God means not hurting myself, and loving this body that God has created. Fearing God means forgiving those who have hurt me. I can't say I've forgiven Chloe totally, but I know with God's help and your support, I can," Stephanie said, gradually breaking into a weak smile.

Dad and Mum gave Stephanie a tight embrace. Soon, the other children piled themselves onto the hug, too.

"Erm . . . It's nice to have a family hug . . . but I'm pretty squashed here . . . " Stephanie said, muffled, trying to catch a whiff of fresh air.

Everyone laughed and playfully huddled around Stephanie again before walking towards the car, hand in hand.

AUTHOR'S NOTE

When my eldest son entered Primary 1 four years ago, I made a difficult decision to leave my full-time job so that I could be home with him after school. I have three boys, and two of them are now in primary school. I always look forward to fetching them from school, as they would eagerly fill me in on their day. Call me self-absorbed, but I am delighted to be the first person to know what makes or breaks their day.

When my eldest son was in Primary 1, I was surprised to discover that I was not ready to tackle some of the issues that he was encountering. One particular incident stuck in my memory.

I was waiting to pick him up from school at my usual spot. That afternoon, when I spotted him and waved, he didn't respond with his usual smile and excitement. In fact, he was looking rather dejected. His hands were shaking, and he walked unsteadily but quickly towards me. When he finally reached me, he immediately embraced me and cried uncontrollably. Everyone in class had to write an appreciation card to their classmates, he said, and a boy whom he considered his "best friend" had crushed the card that he had written to him. Moreover, that boy, who was extremely popular in class, received many cards while my son had none. This and many other incidents prompted me to think about how I could bring my sons up to handle the disappointments, failures, and challenges in life.

Our children are growing up in a trickier world than the one we used to live in, largely due to the influences of the Internet and technology. Sometimes, I do not have an answer to their woes, or I might find myself giving a less-than-ideal response to their questions or situations. Constantly mulling over these situations and thinking about how to help my boys walk wisely, I decided to write this book of 20 short stories exploring real challenges young children face today, and how the Bible, particularly Proverbs, offers insights into how to deal with them. I hope this book can achieve the following purposes:

Encourage parents to engage in honest dialogue with their children about the issues and challenges they face.

Help children see that God's Word is relevant and provides them with wisdom to deal with their challenges.

If you're a parent or caregiver, I encourage you to read these stories with your children, and guide them through the various challenges they face. To help you delve deeper into these issues, some discussion questions and notes for each chapter have been compiled at the end of the book.

Sng Ee Ping

APPENDIX A:
MOBILE PHONE USAGE CONTRACT

MOBILE PHONE USAGE CONTRACT

I know that having a mobile phone is a privilege and responsibility. I respect that my parents love me and want to keep me safe. My parents respect that I am becoming a young adult and want the privilege of having the use of a handphone. With that in mind, we agree to the following:

1. I understand that my parents expect full transparency regarding the content on my phone. They can check my phone any time, and I must share my passwords with them, and notify them if they are changed. I will never message or talk to someone, and then delete or hide it from my parents.

2. Before I join any social media networks or download any app, I will get my parents' permission.

3. I will abide by the limitations on mobile usage set up by my parents.

4.   I will remember the data usage that is allowed by my mobile plan, and not cross the limits of the usage. My parents will pay for the monthly subscription, and I will pay for additional charges if I exceed the limit.

5.   I will respect "device-free time", which include mealtimes and when I am doing my homework. I will ensure that I will not use my phone while crossing the road or in any unsafe way. If I am asked to stop using my phone, I will be happy to do so.

6.   My phone must be turned off by 9 p.m. each school night, and 10 p.m. on other nights. It must be charged in my parents' room.

7.   I will not use my phone to take pictures of nudity, violence, or anything inappropriate or unlawful.

8.   I will not use my phone to call or text anyone for malicious or inappropriate purposes, such as teasing, prank calling, or sexting. I will remember that what I text becomes permanent, and that I should never text something I wouldn't feel comfortable saying directly to a person's face.

9.   I should check with my parents before sharing personal information, such as my

passwords, name, address, phone number, school, etc.

10. I will always have my phone turned on when I am out with friends. I will pick up the phone if one of my parents calls me, and I will always answer texts from my parents, no matter what I am doing or where I am.

11. I will tell my parents immediately if I receive suspicious phone calls or inappropriate text messages.

12. I am responsible for knowing where my phone is, and for keeping it in good condition.

13. I will abide by all these rules. I understand that if they are not followed or if I attempt to circumvent them, there will be consequences, including the loss of my phone privilege.

14. I agree that if I am unable to keep up with my houschold, church, and financial responsibilities, or if I demonstrate untrustworthy behaviour, my phone will be taken away.

15. I agree to memorise a verse every fortnight, so as to grow in wisdom in handling the phone.

Signed (child's name): _________________________________

Signed (parent's name(s)): ________________, ________________

Date: ______________   Date to be reviewed: ______________

DISCUSSION QUESTIONS

CHAPTER 1: Finders Keepers — Proverbs 10:2
THEME: Integrity

1. Share about a time when you wanted something that others had. What did you do about it?
2. How can the riches one gains from sinning be worth nothing?
3. How can doing what is right save you from "death"? What does "death" here mean?

CHAPTER 2: Wisdom and Shame — Proverbs 11:2
THEME: Pride

1. Share a time when others boasted about their abilities or grades. How did you feel? Why did you feel this way?
2. Was there a time when you felt you were better than others? What did you do or say to show you were "better"? What do you think others felt or thought about your words or actions?

3. What can you say to or do for a friend who is not doing as
    well as you in your school, enrichment class, or CCA?

CHAPTER 3: The Trumpet Tree — Proverbs 11:30
THEME: Kindness; being a light

1. Do you know of anyone who has special needs? How are
    they different?
2. How do you and others respond to someone with special
    needs? What are some of the reasons for people reacting to
    them in this way?
3. When you meet someone with special needs for the first
    time, how do you think you can reach out to them in a
    godly way?

CHAPTER 4: Pet Ants — Proverbs 6:6–8
THEME: Teamwork

1. Share a time when you refused to work. What were the
    consequences (for yourself and others) of not doing
    your part?
2. What have you learnt about ants that could help you to be a
    better worker?

CHAPTER 5: Far Richer — Proverbs 11:24
THEME: Giving

1. Without having more money, how can a person be "richer"? What can one do to become "richer"?
2. Is it possible for a person to be "poorer" without having less money? What are some things you do or do not do that might make you "poorer"?

Suggestion to parents: Consider a family project that involves serving the needs of the community, for example, cleaning the house of an elderly, distributing essentials to underprivileged families, etc.

CHAPTER 6: Straight Ahead — Proverbs 15:21
THEME: Bullying

1. Describe a time when you were hurt by the words and actions of someone. What was painful about the experience?
2. How will you respond the next time you are hurt by someone's words and/or actions?

CHAPTER 7: The Gold Ring — Proverbs 11:22
THEME: Body image

1. Share a time when a friend commented on your weight or appearance. How did you feel? Did you want to do something about it?

2. How should you manage your own or your friends' expectations about your appearance?

CHAPTER 8: Body and Bones — Proverbs 14:30
THEME: Jealousy

1. Share a time you were jealous. How did it affect you?
2. How does the understanding of jealousy and fairness help you to relate to situations and/or people this week?

CHAPTER 9: Show-and-Tell — Proverbs 12:18
THEME: Words

1. What are some hurtful words that we should avoid using? How will you remind yourself to be careful about the words you say this week?
2. What are words that bring healing? Think of a friend whom you can speak these words to.

CHAPTER 10: Vinegar and Smoke — Proverbs 10:26
THEME: Laziness

1. Share about a time you were unwilling to help with chores or fulfil your responsibilities. How did your unwillingness affect others?
2. What is a chore that you will help your family with this week?

CHAPTER 11: Do You Like Dogs? — Proverbs 4:26
THEME: Relationships

1. Is there someone you have special feelings for? Has someone indicated his or her interest in you? How do you handle those feelings?
2. What would you look for in a person you want to date? When do you think would be a right time to get into a romantic relationship? Why?

CHAPTER 12: Smashed — Proverbs 14:29
THEME: Anger

1. Share a time when you were quick to anger. What do you think caused your anger? What were the consequences?
2. How can understanding the cause of your anger help you manage your anger in future?

CHAPTER 13: Addiction — Proverbs 14:8
THEME: Gaming addiction

1. Are you addicted to computer games? What other addiction are you currently struggling with?
2. What are the signs of addiction?
3. Why is it important to flee from addiction?

Suggestions to parents: Set boundaries for gaming or phone usage, and frequently review with your children their gaming routines. Plan fun activities that the family can do together. For example, hunt for the best burger in town or go on a cycling trip together. Engage your kids with outdoor activities regularly to encourage them to discover pleasures other than from screen time.

CHAPTER 14: Phone — Proverbs 22:6
THEME: Responsibility

1. What are the purposes of boundaries?
2. What are some things you can do to flee from the temptation of crossing a boundary that has been set for you?

CHAPTER 15: Mr Popular — Proverbs 18:24
THEME: Friendship

1. Do you wish to be popular? Why?
2. Do you have a true friend? How do you know if someone is a true friend?
3. Do you have friends who are popular? What are some reasons for their popularity?

CHAPTER 16: A Dream Come True — Proverbs 14:25
THEME: Justice

1. Will you stand up for someone who has been wronged? Why or why not?

2.   Why is it important to include someone from a different race? What can you do to include them?

CHAPTER 17: See No Evil — Proverbs 22:3
THEME: Online dangers

1.   What are some dangers you might encounter while engaging in online activities?
2.   What are some websites you know of that could be unsafe to enter?
3.   What or whom might be a safe place to run to when you encounter these dangers?

CHAPTER 18: Revelation — Proverbs 25:18
THEME: Cyberbullying

1.   If you are a victim of cyberbullying, how do you deal with hurtful words and comments from friends?
2.   Do you know anyone who is a victim of cyberbullying? What are the consequences?
3.   What are some reasons people turn to self-harm to cope with their negative emotions? Instead of self-harming, what are other ways to cope with our negative emotions (anxiety, anger, resentment, etc.)?

CHAPTER 19: Stephanie — Proverbs 17:22

THEME: Mental wellness; forgiveness

1. Is there someone you need to forgive? Who and why?
2. What makes it difficult to forgive someone?
3. Have you forgiven someone recently? If yes, how did you feel about it?

CHAPTER 20: Reflections — Proverbs 14:27

THEME: Fearing God

1. What are some choices you need to make in order to live wisely?
2. What does it mean to fear the Lord in your life?
3. Which character—Max, Phoebe, Stephanie, or Rick—can you identify with the most? Why?
4. Which topic in this book speaks to you most? How do you want us (parents) to help you?

ABOUT THE PUBLISHER

Discovery House Distributors Singapore is affiliated with Our Daily Bread Ministries.

In support of Our Daily Bread Ministries' mission to make the life-changing wisdom of the Bible understandable and accessible to all, we produce a wide array of premium and quality resources that focus on Scripture, show reverence for God and His Word, demonstrate the relevance of vibrant faith, and equip and encourage you to draw closer to God in all seasons of your life.

NOTE TO THE READER

We invite you to share your response to the message in this book by writing to us at:

5 Pereira Road, #07-01
Asiawide Industrial Building
Singapore 368205
or sending an email to **dhdsingapore@dhp.org**

ABOUT THE AUTHOR

Ee Ping has never dreamed of raising three boys. Raised on a diet of barbie dolls and kitchen toys, she now ventures into a world of transformers, cars, and beyblades. She makes a poor player in a soccer game or a nerf gun battle, but loves to seek out easy cooking recipes to meet their insatiable appetites. When she has a moment alone, she prefers to read and write . . . of course, a durian dessert would perfect her day.